ALL THE THINGS YOU ARE

from VERY WARM FOR MAY

Lyrics by OSCAR HAMMERSTEIN II
Music by JEROME KERN

APRIL IN PARIS

Words by E.Y. HARBURG
Music by VERNON DUKE

BEER BARREL POLKA
(Roll Out The Barrel)
Based on the European success "Skoda Lasky"*

By LEW BROWN, WLADIMIR A. TIMM,
JAROMIR VEJVODA and VASEK ZEMAN

There's a gar - den   what a gar - den   on - ly

hap - py fac - es   bloom there,   and there's nev - er an - y

room there   for a wor - ry   or a gloom there.   Oh, there's

16

BEYOND THE BLUE HORIZON

from the Paramount Picture MONTE CARLO

Words by LEO ROBIN
Music by RICHARD A. WHITING
and W. FRANKE HARLING

22

BOO-HOO

Lyric and Music by EDWARD HEYMAN,
CARMEN LOMBARDO and JOHN JACOB LOEB

25

BLAME IT ON MY YOUTH

Words by EDWARD HEYMAN
Music by OSCAR LEVANT

BLUE HAWAII

from the Paramount Picture WAIKIKI WEDDING

Words and Music by LEO ROBIN
and RALPH RAINGER

Per - fume in the air and rare flow-ers ev-'ry-where, and white shad-ows we could share at Wai - ki - ki. A sky full of

32

33

COCKTAILS FOR TWO

from the Paramount Picture MURDER AT THE VANITIES

Words and Music by
ARTHUR JOHNSTON and SAM COSLOW

CARAVAN
from SOPHISTICATED LADIES

Words and Music by DUKE ELLINGTON,
IRVING MILLS and JUAN TIZOL

FALLING IN LOVE AGAIN
(Can't Help It)
from the Paramount Picture THE BLUE ANGEL

Words and Music by FREDERICK HOLLANDER
Revised Lyric by SAMMY LERNER

EAST OF THE SUN
(And West Of The Moon)

Words and Music by
BROOKS BOWMAN

A FINE ROMANCE
from SWING TIME

Words by DOROTHY FIELDS
Music by JEROME KERN

THE FOLKS WHO LIVE ON THE HILL

from HIGH, WIDE AND HANDSOME

Lyrics by OSCAR HAMMERSTEIN II
Music by JEROME KERN

I CAN'T GET STARTED WITH YOU
from ZIEGFELD FOLLIES

Words by IRA GERSHWIN
Music by VERNON DUKE

HEART AND SOUL
from the Paramount Short Subject A SONG IS BORN

Words by FRANK LOESSER
Music by HOAGY CARMICHAEL

HEARTACHES

Words by JOHN KLENNER
Music by AL HOFFMAN

MCA music publishing

I'LL NEVER SMILE AGAIN

Words and Music by
RUTH LOWE

MCA music publishing

I'M GETTING SENTIMENTAL OVER YOU

Words by NED WASHINGTON
Music by GEORGE BASSMAN

I'M GONNA SIT RIGHT DOWN AND WRITE MYSELF A LETTER

from AIN'T MISBEHAVIN'

Lyric by JOE YOUNG
Music by FRED E. AHLERT

IN A SENTIMENTAL MOOD

Words and Music by DUKE ELLINGTON,
IRVING MILLS and MANNY KURTZ

ISN'T IT ROMANTIC?
from the Paramount Picture LOVE ME TONIGHT

Words by LORENZ HART
Music by RICHARD RODGERS

IT'S THE TALK OF THE TOWN

Words by MARTY SYMES and AL NEIBURG
Music by JERRY LIVINGSTON

Slowly, with expression

JUST ONE MORE CHANCE

Words by SAM COSLOW
Music by ARTHUR JOHNSTON

MOONGLOW

Words and Music by WILL HUDSON,
EDDIE DE LANGE and IRVING MILLS

LAMBETH WALK
from ME AND MY GIRL

Words by DOUGLAS FURBER
Music by NOEL GAY

100

LEANING ON A LAMP-POST
from ME AND MY GIRL

Words and Music by
NOEL GAY

LITTLE GIRL BLUE

from JUMBO

Words by LORENZ HART
Music by RICHARD RODGERS

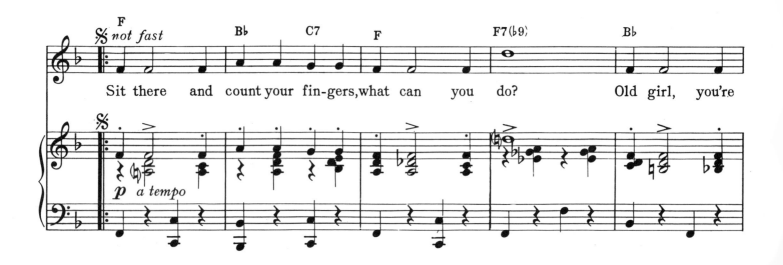

slen-der, Why won't some-bod-y send a ten - der Blue boy to

1.
cheer a lit-tle girl blue?

2.
blue?_____ *Fine*

TRIO

When I was ver-y young _____ the world was young-er than

I, As mer - ry as_____ a car - ou - sel._____

The cir-cus tent was strung _____ with ev - 'ry star in the sky A - bove the ring ___ I loved so well; _____

Now the young world has grown old, _____

Gone are the tin - sel and gold. _____

D.S. al Fine

MY ROMANCE
from JUMBO

Words by LORENZ HART
Music by RICHARD RODGERS

MY VERY GOOD FRIEND, THE MILKMAN

Words by JOHNNY BURKE
Music by HAROLD SPINA

ONE MORNING IN MAY

Words by MITCHELL PARISH
Music by HOAGY CARMICHAEL

PICK YOURSELF UP
from SWING TIME

Words by DOROTHY FIELDS
Music by JEROME KERN

124

PENNIES FROM HEAVEN

Words by JOHN BURKE
Music by ARTHUR JOHNSTON

SOLITUDE

Words and Music by DUKE ELLINGTON,
EDDIE DE LANGE and IRVING MILLS

SEPTEMBER SONG
from the Musical Production KNICKERBOCKER HOLIDAY

Words by MAXWELL ANDERSON
Music by KURT WEILL

SMOKE GETS IN YOUR EYES
from ROBERTA

Words by OTTO HARBACH
Music by JEROME KERN

Lyrics:
They asked me how I knew My true love was true? I of course re-plied, "Some-thing here in-side, Can-not be de-nied." They said some-day you'll find, All who love are blind. When your heart's on

137

SOPHISTICATED LADY

Words and Music by DUKE ELLINGTON,
IRVING MILLS and MITCHELL PARISH

Moderately

They say _____ in - to your

ear - ly life ro-mance came, _____ and in this heart of yours burned a

flame, _____ a flame that flick-ered one day and died a - way.

STARS FELL ON ALABAMA

Words by MITCHELL PARISH
Music by FRANK PERKINS

THANKS FOR THE MEMORY
from the Paramount Picture BIG BROADCAST OF 1938

Words and Music by LEO ROBI
and RALPH RAINGE

146

THESE FOOLISH THINGS
(Remind Me Of You)

Words by HOLT MARVELL
Music by JACK STRACHEY and HARRY LINK

THE TOUCH OF YOUR LIPS

Words and Music by
RAY NOBLE

UNDERNEATH THE ARCHES

Words and Music by
REG CONNELLY, BUD FLANAGAN and JOSEPH McCARTHY

THE VERY THOUGHT OF YOU

Words and Music by
RAY NOBLE

THE WAY YOU LOOK TONIGHT
from SWING TIME

Words by DOROTHY FIELDS
Music by JEROME KERN

YESTERDAYS
from ROBERTA

Words by OTTO HARBACH
Music by JEROME KERN

YOU BROUGHT A NEW KIND OF LOVE TO ME

from the Paramount Picture THE BIG POND

Words and Music by SAMMY FAIN,
IRVING KAHAL and PIERRE NORMAN

than they do— For you've brought a new kind of love to me.

If the sand-man brought me dreams of you— I'd want to sleep my

whole life thru,— For you've brought a new kind of love to me.—

— I know that I'm the slave, you're the queen, But still you can un-der-

WRAP YOUR TROUBLES IN DREAMS
(And Dream Your Troubles Away)

Lyric by TED KOEHLER and BILLY MOLL
Music by HARRY BARRIS

8vb